Incredible Robots in Space

Richard and Louise Spilsbury

raintree

a Capstone company — publishers for children

Raintree is an imprint of Capstone Global Library Limited, a company incorporated in England and Wales having its registered office at 264 Banbury Road, Oxford OX2 7DY – Registered company number: 6695582

www.raintree.co.uk
myorders@raintree.co.uk

Text © Capstone Global Library Limited 2017
The moral rights of the proprietor have been asserted.

Produced for Raintree by Calcium
Edited by Sarah Eason and Amanda Learmonth
Designed by Simon Borrough
Picture research by Susannah Jayes
Production by Victoria Fitzgerald
Originated by Capstone Global Library Ltd © 2016
Printed and bound in India

ISBN 978 1 4747 3122 5 (hardcover)
20 19 18 17 16
10 9 8 7 6 5 4 3 2 1

ISBN 978 1 4747 3200 0 (paperback)
21 20 19 18 17
10 9 8 7 6 5 4 3 2 1

British Library Cataloguing in Publication Data
A full catalogue record for this book is available the British Library.

Acknowledgements
We would like to thank the following for permission to reproduce photographs: Flickr: NASA 34, 35, 40-41, 42, 43; NASA: 1, 5t, 5br, 14, 37br, 44, JPL/University of Arizona 15, JPL-Caltech 22, 28, JPL-Caltech/Space Science Institute 16, JPL/USGS 13; Shutterstock: Elenarts 10, Alexander Smulskiy 7; Wikimedia Commons: Don Davis for NASA 8, NASA 4, 6, 12, 20, 21, 24, 26, 30, 33, 37t, 39, NASA Ames Research Center 9, 45, NASA/JPL 11, 17, 25, NASA/JPL-Caltech 31, NASA/JPL-Caltech/University of Arizona 19, NASA/JPL-Caltech/Malin Space Science Systems 29, Rtphokie 27.

Cover photographs reproduced with permission of: Shutterstock: Alexey Filatov (bg); Wikimedia Commons for NASA: Regan Geeseman (fg).

Design Elements by Shutterstock; nice monkey, (stripes) throughout, phipatbig, (robot) throughout, vlastas, (tech background) throughout.

Contents

Chapter 1

Robots in space

Space exploration is incredibly exciting. One reason people want to explore space is out of curiosity. We want to know what is out there and to find out if there could be **alien** life on any other planets. People also explore space to discover if there are any other planets that humans could live on in the future or that contain useful **resources** we could use on Earth. As the world's population grows and we run out of room in which to live or grow food, the things people discover in space might become very important.

Humans have travelled into space and walked on the Moon, but travel in space puts enormous strain on a human being's body.

Humans in space

The problem with space is that it is a dangerous place for humans to be. Space has no **oxygen** for people to breathe and, away from the rays of the Sun, temperatures plummet to -273 degrees Celsius (-523 degrees Fahrenheit). It is so cold that **molecules** stop moving altogether! **Space shuttles** and spacesuits help protect people from the dangers of space, but even with these technologies, space travel still carries a high level of risk. Yet, without journeying into space, how can we discover more about the wonders of our universe?

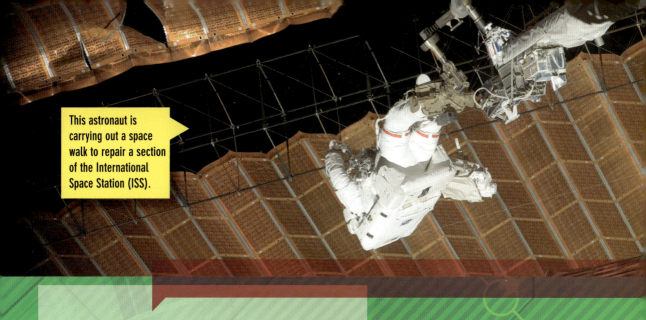

This astronaut is carrying out a space walk to repair a section of the International Space Station (ISS).

Enter the space robot!

Space may be dangerous for humans, but it poses few threats to robots. Robotic astronauts need neither food nor drink to survive in space, and can withstand very inhospitable conditions. Very importantly, although robots are expensive to design and produce, it is far better to lose a robot in space than it is to lose a human. Both the USA's National Aeronautics and Space Administration (NASA) and the European Space Agency (ESA) have developed robots that can travel into space alongside people. One day, these robots may be able to travel into space on their own to find out more about our **galaxy**, and even the realms beyond it.

Human astronauts cannot travel far beyond Earth, but space robots will be able to travel much greater distances – who knows what they may discover!

Probes

A space probe is a robotic spacecraft that is sent into space to do research. Probes travel through space to collect scientific information. There are different types of space probes which collect scientific information about very different environments. Probes gather pictures and data about the planets, moons, **comets** and **asteroids** in our **solar system** as they fly past them. This data is important in helping to plan other space missions, such as voyages to Mars and Saturn. Most probes are not designed to return to Earth, so they make a one-way journey – we could never ask astronauts to do that!

Probes are launched into space by powerful rockets.

Getting into space

Space probes are launched into space on the back of a powerful rocket because spacecraft have to fly at very high speeds to escape the pull of Earth's **gravity**. Once in space, probes separate from the rocket. They then follow a course based on instructions from operators on Earth, as well as instructions that were programmed into them. With no air in space, there is no **air resistance** to slow them down, so the probes keep moving at high speeds. When they reach their destination, the instruments on the probes start taking measurements and sending back this information to Earth by radio. Space probes can carry special cameras, **telescopes** and other instruments far out into the solar system. Many are powered by **solar panels**, which make electricity using energy from the Sun.

The first of many

Sputnik 1 was the first probe to go into space. It was launched on 4 October 1957 by the former Soviet Union. On 31 January 1958, the United States sent a probe called *Explorer 1* into space. Both of these probes studied Earth's upper **atmosphere** from space and made discoveries about what it is like to be in space. A later probe, *Explorer 6*, was launched in August 1959. It took the first pictures of Earth from **orbit**.

The first probe, *Sputnik 1*, was about the size of a beach ball and took 98 minutes to orbit Earth.

Robots are the future

In 2022, the ESA plans to launch a deep-space mission to explore the icy moons of Jupiter. The probe is called *JUICE*, which stands for Jupiter Icy Moons Explorer. It is hoped that *JUICE* will reach Jupiter by 2030. It will spend three or more years studying Jupiter's moons. Information collected by the probe will give us better insight into how **gas giants** and their moons form, and whether these moons could support microscopic life.

7

Pioneers

The *Pioneers* were Earth's first deep-space probes. The first few *Pioneers* were designed to study the Moon, but later versions were launched to study the outer reaches of the solar system. *Pioneer 6*, for example, sent back data about the powerful **solar wind**. When the solar wind reacts with Earth's **magnetic field** and atmosphere, it causes the beautiful displays of dancing lights in the night sky known as **auroras**. *Pioneer 6* was launched in 1965, and continued to send back data to Earth for 35 years, far longer than an astronaut could have survived in space!

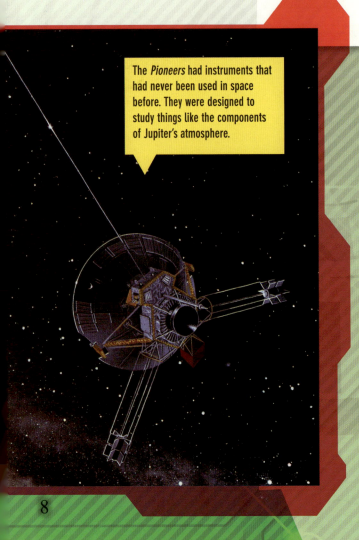

The *Pioneers* had instruments that had never been used in space before. They were designed to study things like the components of Jupiter's atmosphere.

Pioneer 10

In December 1973, after 19 months in space, *Pioneer 10* became the first space probe to fly past Jupiter. Jupiter is more than twice as big as all of the other planets combined, and it has a system of rings and more than 60 moons. One of its moons is bigger than Mercury, and three of them are larger than Earth's moon! *Pioneer 10* discovered Jupiter's magnetic tail, an extension of the planet's **magnetosphere**. After flying past Jupiter, *Pioneer 10* continued towards a distant star called Aldebaran, which it is expected to reach in about 2 million years. In 2003, *Pioneer 10* stopped transmitting data.

Pioneer 11

Launched in 1973, *Pioneer 11* flew past Jupiter in 1974. Its close-up images of Jupiter showed some amazing features, such as a continuous giant storm known as the Great Red Spot. In September 1979, the probe passed within about 21,000 kilometres (13,000 miles) of the planet Saturn. When *Pioneer 11* passed Saturn, it sent the first up-close photographs of the planet to scientists on Earth. It proved that the **asteroid belt** could be safely traversed so that later probes could venture further into space safely. Communication with *Pioneer 11* was lost in 1995.

Robots are the future

The ESA is hoping to launch a space probe called *Don Quijote* in the near future. This space probe will carry out a mission to crash into an asteroid to see if and how the impact changes the course or direction of the asteroid. This could be useful in the future, especially if we ever need to deflect an asteroid to stop it from hitting Earth.

The *Pioneer* probes were the first to send detailed images of Jupiter and Saturn to Earth.

Voyagers 1 and 2

Pioneer 10 held the record for being the furthest human-made object in space until *Voyager 1* overtook it in 1998. *Voyagers 1* and *2* are NASA robot space probes that were designed to observe and transmit more data about Jupiter and Saturn. However, since doing that, they have explored regions of space where no other object from Earth has gone before.

Voyager 1 travels at 57,600 kph (35,800 mph). That is fast enough to travel from Earth to the Sun three and a half times in one year!

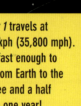

How do they work?

Voyagers 1 and *2* are identical. Each one has equipment to carry out different experiments. These include television cameras, magnetometers for measuring magnetic forces, and **sensors** that can measure the heat of objects as well as detect movement. The *Voyagers* travel too far from the Sun to use solar panels, so they contain devices that convert the heat produced from the natural decay of **plutonium** fuel on the probe into electricity. The information that the probes gather is sent by radio, and signals take about two weeks to reach Earth.

Discoveries

Voyagers 1 and *2* have travelled further than any robots in space. One of the most amazing discoveries from *Voyager 1* was that Jupiter's moon, Io, has active volcanoes. This was the first time active volcanoes had been seen on another body in the solar system. *Voyager 2* also found a thin ring around Jupiter, making it the second planet known to have a ring, and two new moons: Thebe and Metis.

Voyager 2 is the only spacecraft that has visited Uranus and Neptune, and it is the source of a vast amount of our knowledge about those planets. In 2013, *Voyager 1* sent a sound recording to Earth as it left the solar system. This was the first time that we have ever had a recording of sounds in **interstellar** space. Both *Voyager* probes are still sending scientific information about their surroundings. Their current mission is to explore the outermost edge of the Sun's domain and beyond.

Robots are the future

Each *Voyager* probe carries a gold-plated copper disc along with a device to play the disc on and instructions explained in symbols for how to play it. This is so that any aliens finding these spacecraft in the future can see and hear images and sounds that tell them about life on Earth.

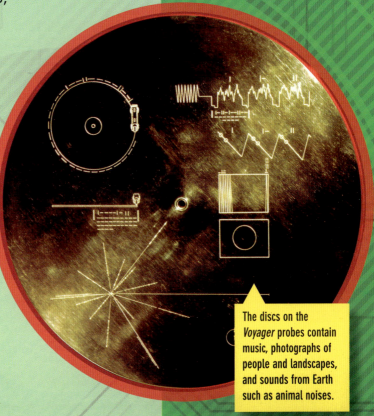

The discs on the *Voyager* probes contain music, photographs of people and landscapes, and sounds from Earth such as animal noises.

Chapter 2

Flying around planets

Some robot spacecraft are designed to orbit, or circle, distant planets or moons to find out more about them. Orbiters can circle an object many times, giving them the chance to make a detailed study of that object. As well as flying further than it is possible for humans to go yet, orbiters also do a job that would be quite dull for people.

The total cost of the *Viking* project was roughly £700 million.

Each *Viking* orbiter had eight solar panels to supply power.

Orbiters at work

A planet exerts a gravitational pull, so a spacecraft would normally be pulled towards the planet when it gets close to it. However, when a robot spacecraft is in orbit, it stays the same height above the surface of a planet, flying on a circular path around it. Orbiters can do this because they are moving so fast. The faster an object travels, the more horizontal distance it covers as it falls, and the gentler the curve of its path – so it ends up circling around and around a planet. Orbiters are usually launched and placed into orbit by rockets.

The Viking orbiters

In 1975, within a few weeks of each other, NASA launched *Viking 1* and *2*. After completing a journey of almost a year, they entered orbits around Mars. The *Viking* orbiters were an octagon shape and measured about 2.5 metres (8.2 feet) across. Each had four wings, measuring almost 10 m (32.8 ft.) from tip to tip. To keep them in the correct orbit, *Viking 1* and *2* carried fuel supplies and had small rockets on top to speed them up or slow them down.

Images of Mars

Each orbiter also had a lander, or landing robotic spacecraft, which landed on the surface of Mars (see pages 18–19). The landers from the *Viking* orbiters were the first robotic spacecraft to transmit pictures from Mars' surface. They took images of almost the entire surface as they circled the planet. These images revealed things like volcanoes, giant canyons, **craters**, landforms created by wind and evidence that there was once water on the Martian surface. The *Viking* orbiters also recorded weather patterns on Mars and took photographs of the planet's two tiny moons, Deimos and Phobos.

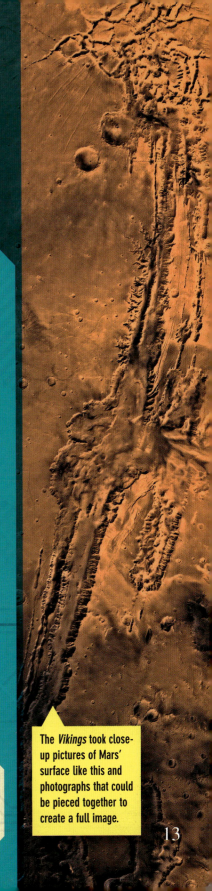

The *Vikings* took close-up pictures of Mars' surface like this and photographs that could be pieced together to create a full image.

13

Galileo: studying Jupiter

In 1989, the orbiter *Galileo* was launched into space. Its task was to take photos of the planet Jupiter, as well as collecting information about its magnetic field and its moons from orbit. It took six years for *Galileo* to travel the 3.7 billion km (2.3 billion mi.) to reach Jupiter's orbit, a journey that a manned spacecraft cannot do yet. So far, no rocket has been created that could take off from Earth's surface and escape its gravitational pull to reach space, while carrying the weight of a large spacecraft, astronauts, supplies and materials needed for such a long journey.

The Space Shuttle carried the *Galileo* spacecraft in its cargo bay.

Slingshot into space

Galileo was launched from the space shuttle *Atlantis*. It travelled to Venus and back to Earth, using the gravity of these planets to fling it, as if from a slingshot, to Jupiter. This technique is called a **gravity assist**. It is used to save a spacecraft time and energy. *Galileo* started working before it arrived at Jupiter, taking pictures of asteroids as it passed through the asteroid belt. It got the first close-up views of the asteroids Gaspra and Ida. At the same time, it discovered a **satellite** orbiting Ida.

Galileo's *mission*

Just before entering Jupiter's orbit, *Galileo* released a probe that dropped slowly by parachute through part of Jupiter's atmosphere. It sent data to *Galileo* about things like the temperature and cloud structure, and measured the amount of water and other chemicals there, before the heat and pressure in the atmosphere broke through its heat shield and destroyed it.

Galileo then proceeded to fly in a series of different orbits around Jupiter, taking close-up pictures of the planet's four moons as well as of Jupiter's clouds, auroras and storms, including the Great Red Spot. After that, *Galileo* was sent into Jupiter's magnetic field to get closer to its innermost moon, Io, to study its active volcanoes. Jupiter's magnetic field is incredibly dangerous — it traps **radiation**, leading to levels that are more than 1,000 times the lethal dose for a human. The powerful radiation damaged *Galileo*. Finally, in September 2003, *Galileo* was instructed to fall into Jupiter's atmosphere and destroy itself.

Galileo took this image of a volcanic region on Io. Io gets its yellow-orange colour from the sulphur given off by the volcanoes.

Orbiters help us understand planets as a whole. They have revealed a wealth of information about Mars.

Cassini: studying Saturn

The orbiter *Cassini* was designed to explore Saturn and its atmosphere, rings, magnetosphere and moons. *Cassini* was launched in 1997 and reached Saturn's orbit seven years later. It was the first robotic spacecraft to orbit Saturn – *Pioneer 11* and *Voyagers 1* and *2* had only flown past.

Cassini is 6.7 m (22 ft.) high and 4 m (13.1 ft.) wide, which is about the same size as a 30-seater bus!

Cassini took detailed pictures of Saturn's moon, Titan.

Cassini *and* Huygens

Although NASA made the *Cassini* orbiter, it carried with it an ESA probe called *Huygens*, which measured 2.7 m (8.9 ft.) across. *Cassini* released *Huygens* on 25 December 2004, and let it drop by parachute towards Titan, Saturn's largest moon. *Huygens* was equipped with six instruments, which it used to study the atmosphere and the surface of Titan. *Huygens* sent data and images back to the orbiter, which *Cassini* then transmitted to Earth.

Cassini's discoveries

After *Cassini* released *Huygens*, it continued to orbit Saturn numerous times and fly by the planet's other moons. *Cassini's* instruments include **radar** to map the cloud-covered surface of Titan, and a magnetometer to study Saturn's magnetic field. *Cassini* took amazing pictures of things like Saturn's cloud patterns, which showed that wind speeds on the planet can reach more than 1,700 km (1,100 mi.) per hour — more than four times the top speed of winds on Earth. Pictures taken by *Cassini* also showed that Saturn's moon Enceladus, which had been thought to be frozen and dead, had **geysers** erupting on it. This helped scientists work out that the geysers create one of Saturn's rings. They also saw water ice in the geysers, which scientists say may mean that Enceladus has an underground ocean and could even have an environment where life is possible. *Cassini* also discovered six new moons and two new rings around Saturn.

Robots are the future

Cassini's orbit will soon be changed so that it will pass inside Saturn's innermost ring and go even nearer to Titan. After making closer orbits, *Cassini's* final mission will end by plunging into Saturn. It is hoped that *Cassini* will be able to tell us something about Saturn's atmosphere, before it is destroyed.

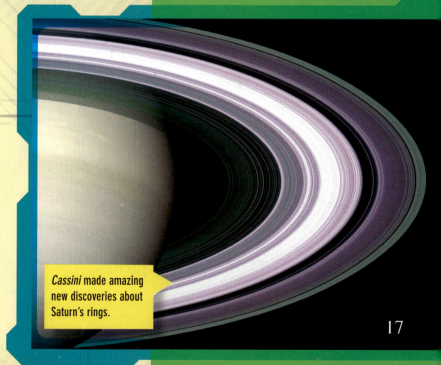

Cassini made amazing new discoveries about Saturn's rings.

Chapter 3

Other worlds

Landers, as their name suggests, are robotic spacecraft designed to touch down on the surface of a moon, planet or other space body. Their job is to collect images and other information about these worlds. In 1975, NASA sent two *Viking* missions to put landers on Mars: *Viking 1* and *Viking 2*. In 1976, almost a year after being launched, NASA's *Viking 1* lander made history when it became the first successful lander to touch down on Mars, at least 56 million km (34.8 million mi.) away from Earth.

The Viking landers

The *Viking* landers flew into space together with their orbiters, but separated and dropped to the planet's surface after entering the orbit around Mars. The dangerous thing for landers is the landing. As the landers pass through the Martian atmosphere, **friction** against the gases in the atmosphere causes dangerously high temperatures of up to 2,093°C (3,800°F). The *Viking* landers had thick heat shields to protect them, and a parachute to slow them down a little for landing and to slightly reduce that friction. Just before landing, three lander legs with honeycomb-shaped aluminium **shock absorbers** were extended to soften the landing.

In 1971, the *Mars 3* lander touched down on Mars. It survived for only a few seconds and sent back no useful data.

Happy landings

The two *Viking* landers touched down on Mars about 6,400 km (4,000 mi.) apart. After landing, they began taking pictures and doing scientific experiments. They analysed the soil and took colour images of the planet's rocky surface and dusty, pinkish sky. The landers did experiments to look for evidence of life in soil samples, but they did not find any traces on the surface of the planet. Each lander went on working much longer than its planned life span of three months after touchdown. *Viking 1* made its final transmission to Earth on 11 November 1982, and the mission officially ended the following year. The mission's most amazing achievement was to send the first pictures of the surface of Mars to Earth. They showed Mars to be a cold planet with reddish volcanic soil, with some evidence of ancient riverbeds.

The *Viking* landers took 4,500 images of the surface of Mars, and over 3 million weather-related measurements were sent back to Earth.

19

Pathfinder

In 1997, a new lander, *Pathfinder*, touched down about 850 km (530 mi.) southeast of where *Viking 1* had landed on Mars. *Pathfinder* had been launched in December 1996 from Cape Canaveral in Florida, United States, and using gravity assist, took only seven months to reach and land on Mars.

A new kind of lander

Pathfinder was a new kind of lander. It was designed to test an innovative way of landing a robotic spacecraft on a planet's surface – using airbags, not unlike the ones you find in a family car, to ensure a soft landing! As *Pathfinder* descended through the atmosphere on its way to the surface of Mars, it stopped itself from dropping too quickly by using a parachute, a heat shield and rockets. Just eight seconds before hitting the surface, the airbags that surrounded the lander opened, and made it look rather like a big bunch of grapes. The airbags cushioned the fall of the lander and allowed it to bounce safely several times along the surface, until finally coming to rest. In fact, *Pathfinder* was the first robotic spacecraft to bounce on another planet!

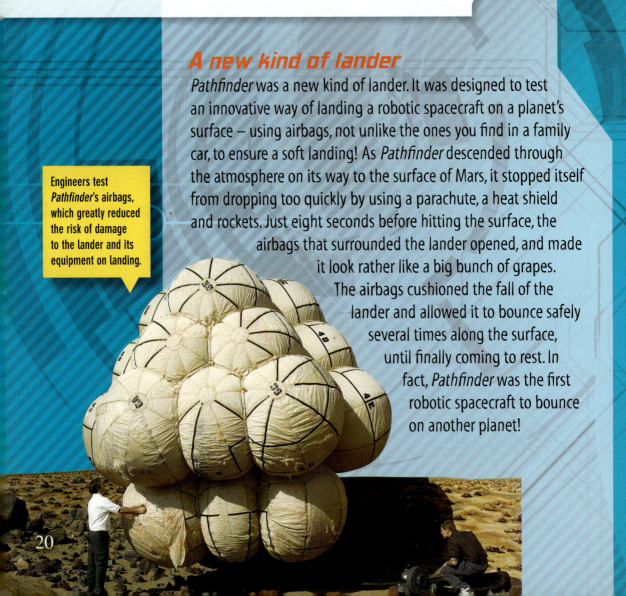

Engineers test *Pathfinder*'s airbags, which greatly reduced the risk of damage to the lander and its equipment on landing.

Pathfinder's *mission*

Pathfinder was a **tetrahedron** shape, with three sides and a base, and it stood almost 1 m (3 ft.) tall. Its main mission was to prove that a cost-effective lander could be sent to Mars, and it also sent back useful information. After landing, it unfolded to reveal the scientific instruments inside. These included magnets, thermometers, wind socks for checking the wind direction and other equipment for investigating the atmosphere on Mars. It sent back 8.5 million different measurements and its camera system sent back more than 16,500 images that gave a vivid view of the surface of Mars. *Pathfinder* transmitted its last data on 27 September 1997.

Robots are the future

Over time, landers have used different methods of getting safely through the atmosphere of Mars and landing on its surface. Each time a lander goes to Mars, designers and engineers on Earth learn more about how to make spacecraft that can do this safely. They are using this knowledge to design a spacecraft that could land people safely on Mars.

Sky Crane

In 2012, a new kind of robotic lander was invented: *Sky Crane. Sky Crane* was designed to lower a very heavy new robot, called *Curiosity* (see pages 28–29), onto Mars to explore the planet's surface. *Sky Crane* was designed to land and deliver *Curiosity* safely, despite passing through the atmosphere of Mars at a potentially deadly 21,000 km (13,000 mi.) per hour.

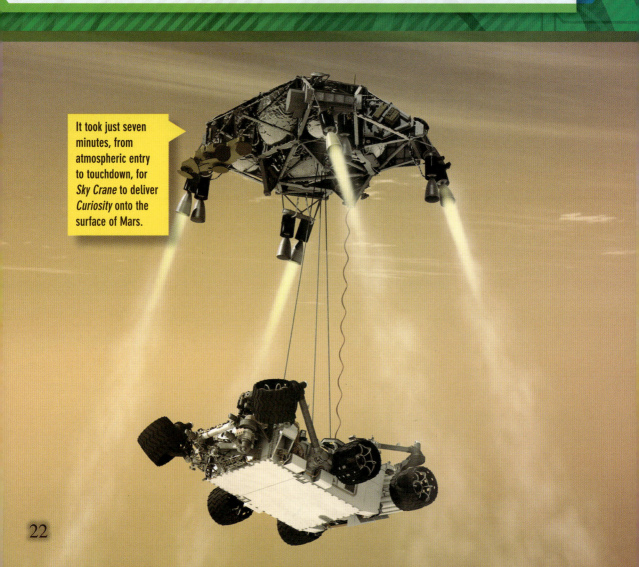

It took just seven minutes, from atmospheric entry to touchdown, for *Sky Crane* to deliver *Curiosity* onto the surface of Mars.

Ready for action!

Sky Crane was like a giant, eight-rocket jetpack. As it descended towards Mars, friction with the atmosphere slowed *Sky Crane* to about 1,600 km (1,000 mi.) per hour. Heat shields prevented the 2,093°C (3,800°F) temperatures caused by this friction from harming the *Sky Crane*. A parachute 18 m (60 ft.) wide, attached to the capsule by cables almost 49 m (160 ft.) long, slowed the *Sky Crane* even more. Lower in the atmosphere, when it was safe to dump the heat shield, *Sky Crane* slowed to about 320 km (200 mi.) per hour.

Mission accomplished

The parachute was cut off, and *Sky Crane* fired its rockets to slow its descent to just 2.4 km (1.5 mi.) per hour. Once within about 18 m (60 ft.) of the surface of Mars, *Sky Crane* lowered *Curiosity* 6 m (20 ft.) beneath it on three nylon ropes. It continued its slow descent until *Curiosity* was resting on the surface. Then the bolts holding *Curiosity* to the *Sky Crane* exploded, separating the two and leaving *Curiosity* to do its job. Having completed its mission, *Sky Crane* then flew out of reach and crashed into the surface of Mars, destroying itself.

Robots are the future

Could *Sky Crane* technology be the key to the future? Landing large spacecraft using rockets, which work by **thrusting** downwards to force the spacecraft upwards, blasts up a lot of dust from the surface, and this could damage the spacecraft. By kicking up dust and soil from the surface, the rockets could also create craters that could cause problems for vehicles as they try to land. Airbags big enough to soften a landing would be too heavy or expensive. In the future, perhaps robotic *Sky Cranes* could be used to land spacecraft carrying humans and their supplies on planets including Mars.

Exploring the surface

Landers can touch down on a planet's surface, but they cannot move around once they get there. This means that they can analyse or take pictures of a limited area of ground. However, the rovers that the landers carry with them and release onto the surface can move around and send back data, often via their landers. Like the orbiters and landers before them, the great advantage of the robot rovers over human astronauts is that they can detect changes in light and energy around them by picking up different **wavelengths**. The rovers can sense things about magnetic fields or microscopic bits of dust that people cannot.

In 1972, during the *Apollo 17* mission, astronauts used a rover to make a short trip on the Moon's surface, but rovers that go further into space are unmanned robots.

The Sojourner *rover*

The day after it landed on the surface of Mars, the *Pathfinder* lander released a six-wheeled, **remote-controlled** rover called *Sojourner*. *Sojourner* was 61 centimetres (2 feet) long, 45.7 cm (1.5 ft.) wide, and 30.5 cm (1 ft.) tall, and weighed around 10 kilogrammes (23 pounds) — about as big as an average microwave oven! It rolled down landing ramps on the side of *Pathfinder* and started its slow progress across the surface. Its maximum speed was 61 cm (2 ft.) per minute. Solar panels and batteries powered *Sojourner*. It had two black-and-white cameras on top that took images of where it was going. *Pathfinder* also sent back images of *Sojourner's* progress, to help scientists decide where to send it. People on Earth used a computer to steer *Sojourner*. They sent instructions to *Pathfinder*, which in turn relayed them to *Sojourner*.

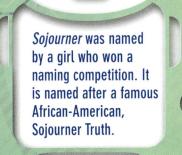

Sojourner was named by a girl who won a naming competition. It is named after a famous African-American, Sojourner Truth.

Sojourner was designed to travel steadily across Mars's rocky surface.

Sojourner's *mission*

Over a period of two and a half months, *Sojourner* travelled 0.48 km (0.3 mi.) away from *Pathfinder*. It took 550 colour photographs and analysed soil and rocks at more than 16 different sites near *Pathfinder*. Data collected by *Sojourner* and transmitted back to Earth by *Pathfinder* showed scientists that rocks on Mars were like some volcanic rocks found on Earth. These, along with information collected by robotic spacecraft, added to evidence suggesting that at some point in the past, Mars was much more like Earth than it is today, with a warmer, thicker atmosphere and water in its liquid state.

Opportunity

Opportunity is a NASA rover that was launched in 2003 and released by its lander onto the surface of Mars in January 2004. Opportunity is a six-wheeled robot equipped with a variety of instruments. These include a camera that can take close-up images of rocks, and rock-grinding tools and other equipment that analyse the rocks, soil and dust on the surface of the planet. Its mission was designed to last 90 days, but ever since Opportunity landed in a crater, it has explored several other craters, and continues to explore today.

Opportunity weighs 174.2 kg (384 lbs.) It measures 1.6 m (5.2 ft.) long and is 1.5 m (4.9 ft.) high.

Mars roving

Like *Sojourner*, *Opportunity* receives instructions about where to move from the Jet Propulsion Laboratory (JPL). The JPL is the NASA command control centre and is about 200 million km (125 million mi.) away from Mars here on Earth. *Opportunity's* six large wheels have thick treads to provide grip to prevent it slipping on sand as it climbs in and out of craters. Each wheel also has its own motor to move the rover in all directions. *Opportunity* runs on solar power, but it does not need a lot of energy because the thin atmosphere on Mars offers far less air resistance than there is on Earth. This means that the rover does not have to **accelerate** much to move. *Opportunity* also has a **suspension system** to help it avoid tipping over. The wheels are connected to the rover body in a way that absorbs some of the impact when the rover hits a bump.

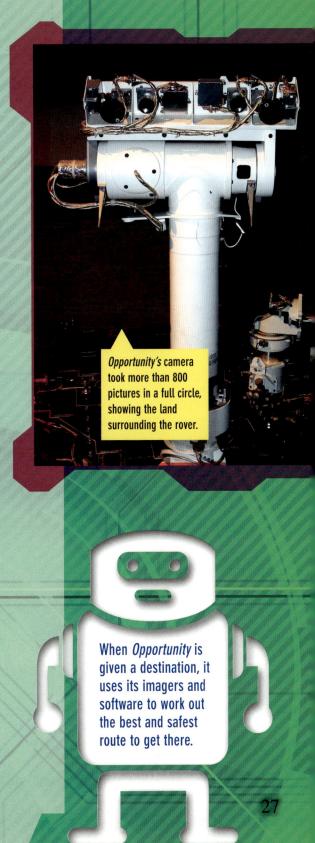

Opportunity's camera took more than 800 pictures in a full circle, showing the land surrounding the rover.

Setbacks and successes

Despite a few problems — *Opportunity* was stuck in a sand dune and dust storms threatened to clog its solar panels — this rover has travelled more than 40 km (25 mi.) on Mars, setting a new off-Earth driving record. It has also made some interesting discoveries. For example, it found evidence of past water and rocks that may have been part of the shoreline of an ancient body of salty water.

When *Opportunity* is given a destination, it uses its imagers and software to work out the best and safest route to get there.

Curiosity

The *Curiosity* rover, which was lowered onto the surface of Mars by the *Sky Crane*, is about 2.7 m (9 ft.) long. It weighs about 900 kg (2,000 lbs.), which is around four times as heavy as *Opportunity*. *Curiosity* cost £2 billion to build and is the longest, heaviest rover on Mars. It is capable of exploring a far greater area than any Mars rover before it. *Curiosity* is equipped like a mobile science laboratory, so it can find out if living things were ever able to live on the planet or if they could in the future. It was launched by rocket from Cape Canaveral in November 2011, and it landed in the Gale Crater on Mars in August 2012.

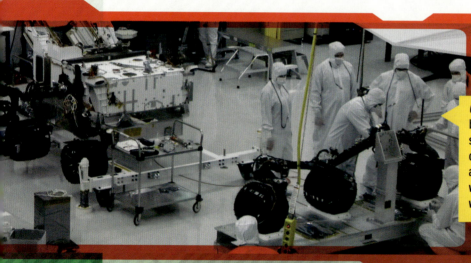

Curiosity's engineers built its suspension system so it can climb over obstacles twice as high as its wheels, while keeping all six wheels on the ground.

Curiosity *stats and facts*

It takes about 90 people, based at the JPL, to operate a Mars rover. *Curiosity* generates its power using heat from the natural decay of plutonium. Its wheels have a diameter of 50.8 cm (20 in.) and its robotic arm is 2.1 m (7 ft.) long. Its suspension system helps it roll over rocks and other obstacles up to 73 cm (29 in.) high and to travel an average of 30 m (98 ft.) per hour.

Discoveries

The *Curiosity* rover can travel up to 19 km (12 mi.) and has used its instruments to study rocks and soils to see what it was like on Mars in the past. *Curiosity* has made several important discoveries. In September 2012, it took pictures of gravel that had been **eroded** by water, suggesting that Gale Crater was once the site of an ancient stream. It also found that in the past, Mars could have had an atmosphere that supported life. However, it found no evidence of methane in the air (methane gas is a sign of life) and it found radiation levels that could pose health risks to astronauts.

Robots are the future

Curiosity has shown that we can safely land a very heavy, large robotic spacecraft on the surface of Mars and at a fairly specific site. Scientists believe that in the near future, a rover might be able to do a return mission and bring back rocks and soils to Earth. This would allow scientists to study them in a laboratory.

In October 2012, *Curiosity* took 55 "selfies", which were pieced together to create this full-colour image of the rover on Mars.

Studying Mars

Scientists are especially interested in Mars because it is the planet that most resembles our own. It has a solid, rocky surface, and seasons and days as long as those on Earth. Although it is very cold, it would be more hospitable than a planet like Venus, which is burning hot and has a poisonous atmosphere.

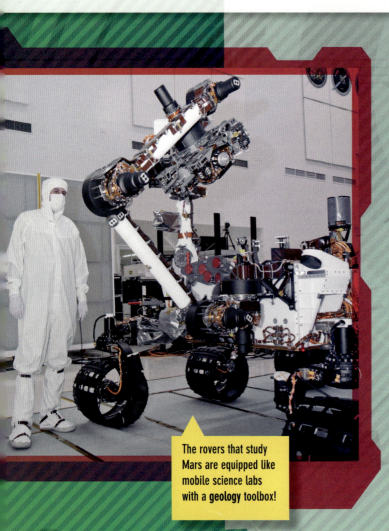

The rovers that study Mars are equipped like mobile science labs with a **geology** toolbox!

Travelling to Mars

Human travel to Mars is impossible today because a rocket big enough to carry all the fuel and supplies needed for the journey would not be able to take off. However, discoveries made by rovers and other robotic spacecraft could help us find ways of travelling and living there in the future. To study Mars, the rovers we send there have a variety of different tools and equipment.

Rover tools

Rovers are designed to look for and find interesting rocks and soils, and then to move to those areas and study them. They have a robotic arm that holds and adjusts several instruments. The arm can reach towards a rock and use a hand-like structure at the end of the arm, which is shaped like a cross, to hold different tools at different angles. These tools include:

Curiosity has a camera on top of a mast on its head that is made up of two "eyes" (lenses). This camera can take colour pictures. It also has **filters** that help scientists analyse rocks and decide whether to send the rover to check out those samples.

▶ A spectrometer. Many of the rocks on Mars contain iron, so there is a lot of iron in the soil, too. This device tests exactly how much and what type of iron is in a sample.

▶ A rock abrasion tool. This grinder can drill a hole about 5 cm (2 in.) in diameter and 5 millimetres (0.2 in.) deep into rock for samples.

▶ A microscopic imager. This is a microscope and a camera that takes close-up and very detailed pictures of rocks and soils.

▶ An APX spectrometer. This analyses the chemicals that make up rocks and soils using **X-rays**.

Robots are the future

One reason scientists study how much iron there is in surface rocks on Mars is because they believe that one day, they might be able to send up machines to extract rock containing iron. They could then turn this iron ore into metal that could be used to build machines, shelters and other structures that people need.

chapter 5

Robotic arms

Rovers rely on robotic arms to carry equipment, for example, to take samples or to see where they are going. On Earth, robotic arms are used for a wide range of purposes. Some arms spray-paint or weld pieces of metal together to make new cars. Others are used by surgeons to perform delicate operations or by soldiers to detect and explode bombs or mines. Whatever their use, and whatever tools they carry, most arms work in similar ways.

What is a robotic arm?

A robotic arm is made up several parts, rather like a human arm. It has several long, stiff pieces or links, like our long bones. These are connected and moved relative to each other by **joints** that are usually rotary joints, like our shoulder joints. There are other types of joints, too, such as joints that slide two long pieces together or apart in the same direction. Each joint is powered by an electric motor. This provides the force to rotate or extend the links to or from each other. Our arms move our hands to the position where they need to work or do something, such as feed us or operate a joystick. The wrist joint and finger joints then operate the hand. This is the same in robotic arms, where the arm is called a manipulator because it positions the "hand", or end effector. The end effector's job is to position and operate a variety of tools connected to the "wrist" joint.

Space crane

One of the simplest arms in space is found on the Russian part of the ISS. Called the Strela Crane, this telescopic pole can extend up to 14 m (46 ft.) and is attached by a rotary joint. It is used to move large, bulky objects from one place to another on the ISS, like unloading cargo from spacecraft. Unlike arms in use in space today, the Strela is not powered. It has to be extended or shortened using a hand crank, which is tiring for astronauts. However, as there is no need to plug in the arm, it can be located anywhere on the ISS using a second Strela.

The ISS Strela Cranes are operated by spacewalkers outside the station, rather than from a console inside the ISS.

The Strela Cranes are used to move astronauts and components around the outside of the ISS.

Canadarm

In November 1981, the second-ever space shuttle mission, STS-2, took the robotic arm known as *Canadarm* into space for the first time. It soon became the workhorse of the shuttle programme and was used up to the final shuttle mission in 2011.

Jobs for Canadarm

Canadarm had two shoulder joints, one at the elbow and three at the wrist. It had a grabber end effector. The arm could stretch out to 15 m (50 ft.) long and by gripping a metal beam, it could reach even further so that astronauts could inspect and mend damage at any point on the shuttle. *Canadarm* not only shifted cargo but could also hold up astronauts away from the shuttle, for example, to mend objects such as the **Hubble Space Telescope**. The arm was fixed into the shuttle's hold and could unfold once the payload doors were opened.

Canadarm is a remote-controlled mechanical arm that can bend and turn with more flexibility than even a human arm!

Canadarm's *vital stats*

The arm was hollow and weighed 408 kg (900 lbs.) on Earth. Although it could not support its own weight on Earth, it could do that and lift more than 265,800 kg (586,000 lbs.) in the **microgravity** conditions in space. Heavy objects carried by the shuttle were usually large and could damage the shuttle, especially when being unloaded from the cargo bay. Astronauts trained for many hours on Earth to learn how to control the sensitive joystick that moved *Canadarm*. It was accurate enough to put a peg in a hole with fewer than 0.2 cm (0.1 in.) clearance. This accuracy proved very useful, for example, to knock ice from a shuttle vent that was clogged with frozen wastewater.

Improved Canadarm

Engineers have built a new and improved *Canadarm* to work on the ISS. Today's *Canadarm2* is a longer, heavier version of the *Canadarm* that was first used on the ISS in 2001. Its greater power gives it the ability not only to help visiting spacecraft to dock, but also to unload components and assemble them into new parts of the ISS. Unlike the original *Canadarm*, *Canadarm2* can move around! There are several ports around the ISS that either end of the arm can plug itself into to get power and link to the controller. Another improvement is that *Canadarm2* can walk rather like a looping caterpillar by connecting a free end to the next port, then releasing the fixed end from its starting port, and so on.

Canadarm is used to deploy, capture and repair satellites, position astronauts and move cargo.

Dextre: space oddjobber

In 2008, a new robot started work on the ISS. *Dextre*'s job was to perform a range of routine tasks that normally would have to be done by astronauts on **spacewalks**. Getting a robot to do the work frees up time for the astronauts, giving them a chance to stay on the ISS to conduct experiments. There are many typical chores for *Dextre*. These include replacing the dead batteries used to store power on the ISS, opening and closing covers, connecting cables and changing fuses. Occasional tasks in its job description include helping to carry out scientific experiments and testing new tools.

Dextre is operated by controllers at NASA's Johnson Space Center and the Canadian Space Agency in Quebec.

All in a day's work

Dextre is a robot hand much bigger than a person. It has two arms measuring more than 3.7 m (12 ft.) long, each with seven joints. The arms can move side to side, down and up, rotate and bend backwards. Each joint is sealed to prevent grease floating off into space. Each arm is tipped with an end effector like a multi-tool. It contains a powered socket spanner, a camera and lights so that astronauts on ISS can see what it is doing, and a plug-in power connector. There are also sensors so that it can detect how much force to use, for example in moving accurately to a particular position, in gripping an object or in tightening bolts without breaking them. *Dextre* can move on the spot, working all around where it is located.

This picture of *Dextre*, also known as the Special Purpose Dextrous Manipulator (SPDM), was taken by a crew member on the ISS.

Space railway

Canadarm2 and *Dextre* are part of a mobile servicing system on the ISS. A third robot completes the system. This is a moveable base to which the two arms attach, which can slide on rails from one end of the ISS to the other. This base can support both arms, plus the weights they are carrying, and move them more quickly and easily around the station on the space railway. The base can also transport astronauts and their tools. It has inbuilt cameras to view the exterior of the ISS and the arms in action.

Dextre can ride on the end of *Canadarm2* or on the Mobile Base System to move from worksite to worksite.

37

Chapter 6

Robonaut· astronaut of the future

On the ISS, *Robonaut* (a robotic astronaut) is helping human astronauts with their work. *Robonaut* is a new kind of robot. It is not just a useful machine that can do work usually done by humans – it looks a little like a human, too! It is the size of a human in a spacesuit and it has a head, body, arms and hands. Its head has cameras that work a little like human eyes!

Robot hands

Robonaut is designed to do tasks that could normally be done only by humans, not robots. To do this it needs to be able to use "hands" to do work. The challenge for the robotics development team was to build a machine with the amazing levels of **dexterity**, movement and strength of a human being. With *Robonaut*, they achieved this. *Robonaut's* hands move like human hands and, with the help of the ISS team, *Robonaut* posted its first social media message via a smartphone on 26 July 2010!

Robonaut can do many things, including using the same tools as an astronaut.

Useful R2

Robonaut 1 was built and designed at NASA's Johnson Space Center in Houston, Texas, USA. It was tested in the laboratory but never left the ground. *Robonaut 2*, also known as *R2*, was an improved version and in 2011, the space shuttle *Discovery* launched this robot's head, upper body and arms to the ISS. At first, *R2* did not really do anything useful. It simply took part in a number of experiments to check its ability to push buttons, flip switches and use tools that human astronauts normally operate. However, *R2* learns as it does things, and it is becoming more and more useful!

Robots are the future

Robonaut is currently used only inside the ISS, but NASA hopes that *Robonaut* will one day be tested outside the Station. If tests are successful, a robot astronaut may even journey to planets beyond our own solar system in the future.

Robonaut *in action*

At the moment, *Robonaut* is using its capabilities to do dull, repetitive tasks on the ISS, which is a common use for robots everywhere. For example, it acts as a cleaner, wiping down surfaces and cleaning handrails, as well as doing other boring tasks such as monitoring air flow from vents. In 2014, after months of being tested on the ground, a pair of legs was launched to the ISS and attached to *R2* in August that same year. The next stage is for *Robonaut* to learn to use these legs and for astronauts to test *Robonaut* to see how useful it can be in space. Its amazing legs are just one part of the robonaut's body that make this robot so special.

The neck can turn and bend so that *Robonaut* can look up, down, left and right.

The backpack holds *R2's* power system.

There is no room in its head for a "brain", so the robot's powerful computer processors are housed in its stomach.

Robonaut has used sign language to say hello to the world. It was also the first humanoid to shake hands in space!

R2's legs are not like human legs. They have seven joints to make them very flexible. They can stretch out to a length of 2.7 m (9 ft.) Instead of feet they have clamping devices that can grip handrails and other objects, leaving *R2's* hands free to do work. There are cameras in the feet, so it will be able to "see" where it is going.

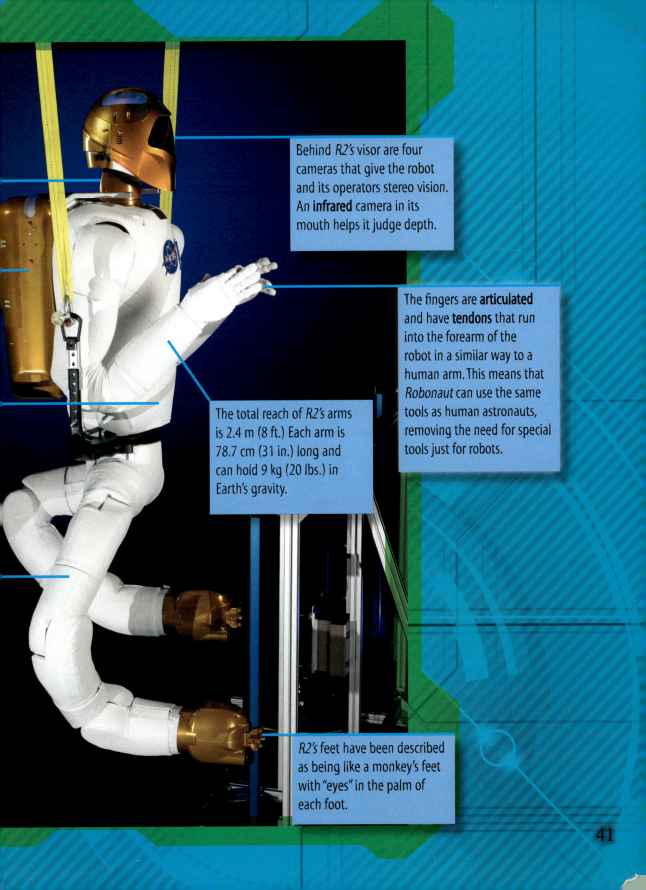

Behind *R2*'s visor are four cameras that give the robot and its operators stereo vision. An **infrared** camera in its mouth helps it judge depth.

The fingers are **articulated** and have **tendons** that run into the forearm of the robot in a similar way to a human arm. This means that *Robonaut* can use the same tools as human astronauts, removing the need for special tools just for robots.

The total reach of *R2*'s arms is 2.4 m (8 ft.) Each arm is 78.7 cm (31 in.) long and can hold 9 kg (20 lbs.) in Earth's gravity.

R2's feet have been described as being like a monkey's feet with "eyes" in the palm of each foot.

Controlling Robonaut

Robonaut performs its functions in two ways. It comes loaded with a set of commands that tell it how to do certain tasks by itself. An operator keeps an eye on what it is doing so that corrections can be made while *R2* is working. *Robonaut* can also be remote controlled, either by an astronaut on the ISS or by an operator at mission control on Earth.

Copy-cat Robonaut

The person who controls *R2* from the ground wears a **virtual-reality** face helmet and gloves. The helmet is remotely linked to the robot's head, so the operator can see what the robot sees. When the operator moves his or her head and neck, *R2* does the same. The gloves are remotely linked to *R2's* hands. When the operator wants *R2* to pick up something, he or she uses its cameras to find and identify the object, then reaches out and grabs it, which makes the robot reach for it, too. One of the problems with controlling *R2* from far away is that signals take time to transmit over long distances. Signals between Earth and the ISS take a couple of seconds to get there, and sometimes they cut out completely. Astronauts on the ISS control *R2* through keyboard commands on a laptop. One astronaut even managed to make *R2* catch a floating roll of tape inside a laboratory on the ISS.

Engineers work closely with robonauts to improve their skills.

Robonaut's **operators see what** *Robonaut* **sees on live video from the head cameras behind its helmet.**

A careful worker

ISS operators on the ground and astronauts on the Space Station have been testing *R2's* dexterity by making the robot work with flexible things like space blankets. When the robot touches an object, tiny sensors on its fingers measure the amount of force being used. This helps *Robonaut* do delicate jobs that most robots, which have to be perfectly lined up next to a target to do their job, cannot do. *Robonaut* can feel its way on a job, checking, for example, that a peg is lined up properly in a hole and moving it slightly until it is, before hammering it into place.

Robots are the future

At the moment *Robonaut* can be powered only through an extension cord connected to the ISS's electrical supply, A power backpack is being developed and tested so that *Robonaut* will soon be able to move longer distances and roam outside the ISS on its own.

Space robots of the future

In the future, *R2* will be able to move around outside the ISS and other spacecraft. Astronauts go on spacewalks like this to set up science experiments, make repairs or test new equipment. They also do spacewalks to extend the ISS. Humans can go outside a spacecraft for a limited time only, and they may not always be able to cope in an emergency. *R2* will be able to stay out much longer as it does not need to break for food or sleep. It can also respond to emergencies.

Other robonauts

Robonaut 2 is not the only robonaut. There are four others and more in the development stages. In the future, these robonauts could be fitted with wheels or jetpacks. Robonauts with wheels would be able to drive across the Moon and Mars, and robonauts with jetpacks could explore space. Another major innovation for the future is to train robonauts to take the place of human doctors and nurses so they can perform routine and life-saving operations. NASA is training a robonaut to do medical tasks like finding a pulse and giving an injection.

NASA is developing a spider-like robot called Spidernaut to carry increasingly heavy loads across uneven planet surfaces.

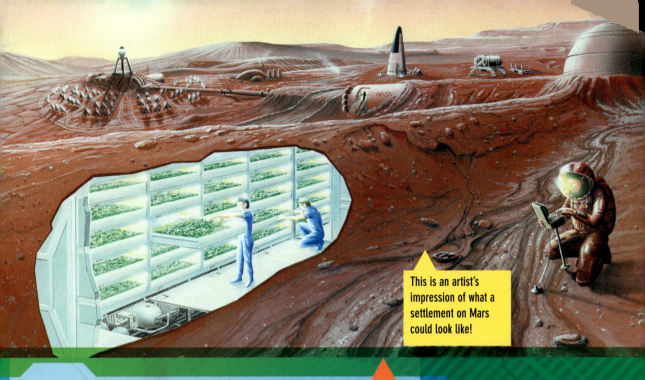

This is an artist's impression of what a settlement on Mars could look like!

How robots help

Creating robots that work in space not only helps us learn more about the world beyond our own planet, but it also means people can use the technology to create humanoid robots to help us with tasks on Earth. As robonauts develop the skills to work in places that would be too dangerous for humans in space, they could also be used to help us in unsafe places on Earth, such as near volcanoes or in nuclear power stations. Technologies developed for robonauts could also be used to improve or make new robots for the armed forces or factories, and for underwater exploration. Robots created to heal astronauts in space could also be used to treat people here on Earth!

Robots are the future

In spite of the advantages of using robots in space, some people question whether they could ever replace humans. They say that although astronaut missions are more dangerous and expensive than robot missions, robots will do only what they are programmed to do, while people will notice things that were previously unknown. What do you think?

Glossary

accelerate increase speed

air resistance force that slows down the movement of an object through the air

alien being from another world

articulated having two or more sections connected by a flexible joint

asteroid belt area of space between the orbits of Mars and Jupiter where most asteroids are found

asteroid small rocky body that orbits the Sun; most asteroids are found between the orbits of Mars and Jupiter

atmosphere layer of different gases that surrounds a planet or moon

aurora pattern of colourful, dancing lights in a planet's atmosphere

comet ball of rock and ice that orbits the Sun; it has a long, bright tail when it passes near the Sun

crater large dip in a planet's surface, caused by the impact of another object

dexterity the ability to use hands skillfully

erode wearing away of rock or soil by wind, water or ice

filter device that allows only some kinds of light to pass through it

friction force occurring when two surfaces rub against each other, creating some heat

galaxy one of the very large groups of stars that make up the universe

gas giant one of four large planets – Uranus, Jupiter, Neptune and Saturn – that is made mainly from gases

geology study of rocks and soil

geyser underground spring that shoots out hot water and steam through a hole in the ground

gravity force that pulls two objects together

gravity assist when a spacecraft uses the gravity of a planet to speed up, slow down or change direction

Hubble Space Telescope space telescope in orbit around Earth

infrared rays of light that cannot be seen by human eyes

interstellar between the stars; most often used to describe travel from one star to another

joint place where two things or parts, such as bones, are joined

magnetic field area near a magnetic body where the magnetic force can be felt

magnetosphere magnetic field extending into space around a planet or star

microgravity condition of weightlessness in space

molecule smallest possible amount of a particular substance that has all the characteristics of that substance

orbit path one object in space takes around another

oxygen gas in the air that living things need to breathe

plutonium radioactive substance that is used to make nuclear energy

radar device that uses radio waves to find out the position of an object

radiation rays of energy given off by radioactive elements

remote control device used to operate a machine from a distance

resource supply of something useful, such as air, water or fuel

satellite electronic device placed in orbit around Earth, used to gather and send information

sensor device that detects changes such as heat or movement

shock absorber device that reduces the effect of travelling over a bumpy surface

solar panel panel that uses the energy in sunlight to make electricity

solar system the Sun and the planets, and other objects that move around it

solar wind electrically and magnetically charged particles sent out from the Sun

space shuttle reusable spacecraft that can carry people and cargo between Earth and space

spacewalk period of time during which an astronaut leaves the spacecraft to move around in space

suspension system system of springs and shock absorbers that help a vehicle absorb the shock of bumps as it drives across rough ground

telescope instrument made of lenses and mirrors that is used to view distant objects

tendon part of the body that connects a muscle to a bone

tetrahedron flat-sided solid object with four faces

thrusting pushing with a lot of force

virtual reality artificial world created by a computer that is controlled by the person who is experiencing it

wavelength distance between two peaks of a wave

X-ray invisible ray of light that can pass through an object to see inside it

Find out more

Books

Rockets and Space Travel (It'll Never Work: An Accidental History of Inventions), Jon Richards (Franklin Watts, 2016)

Space (Research on the Edge), Angela Royston (Wayland, 2014)

Space Exploration (DK Eyewitness), DK editors (Dorling Kindersley, 2014)

Welcome to Mars, Buzz Aldrin (National Geographic Kids, 2015)

Websites

Watch this video clip of NASA space robot, Valkyrie:
www.bbc.co.uk/newsround/36207742

FInd out all about the ESA here:
www.esa.int/esaKIDSen

Design your own rover and play this fun game:
www.sciencemuseum.org.uk/online_science/ games/rugged-rovers

Index